The Dance of Intimacy

The Dance of Intimacy:
love, loss & longing through poetry

Linda Wall

Fourth Dimension Publishing
Kamloops, BC
Canada

The Dance of Intimacy: love, loss & longing through poetry

© Copyright 2007, Linda Wall

ISBN 978-0-9732282-0-5
Third printing

Fourth Dimension Publishing
Kamloops, BC

Library and Archives Canada Cataloguing in Publication

Wall, Linda, 1956-2024
    The dance of intimacy: love, loss & longing through poetry / Linda Wall.

Also available in electronic format and on audio CD.
ISBN 978-0-9732282-0-5

    1. Love poetry, Canadian (English). I. Title.
PS8645.A4665D35 2007   C811'.6   C2007-901808-4

All poems in this collection are written by Linda Wall, except the following which were written to and for Linda by Albert Miller: 'The Bandit's Warning,' 'The Diamond Rose in My Heart,' 'Your Heart You Say!!!?!?,' 'The Grizzly Goddess,' 'Love Is Like a Rose,' 'The Goddess's Web,' and 'My Spirit Longs For Your Embrace.' Copyright © 1995, Albert Lee Miller.

All rights reserved. No part of this book may be reproduced or used in any form or by any means, electronic or mechanical, including photocopying, recording, or by any information retrieval system, without permission in writing from the author. Except for brief excerpts for review.

                1st printing 2007
                2nd printing 2019
                3rd printing 2026

Dedicated To

Eros and Venus

Heart of a Poet

Ah—the heart of a poet
    the lovers' best friend.
Don't get me wrong
    I sing love's song,
but all is not well
    in Lovers' Land.
Sometimes it can be
down right hell,
    and this I write of too.

Table of Contents

Foreword .... *xi*
Preface .... *xii*
Acknowledgments .... *xiii*
A Word Before .... *xiv*

The Dance of Intimacy
   The Dance of Intimacy 17
   I'm Afraid 18
   Choices In the Garden 19
   I'm so Tired 20
   This Robed Gift 22
   Teddy Bears 24
   The Friendship Candle 25
   The Heart is a Betrayer of the Mind 26
   Pain Filled Soul 27
   My Erotic Fantasy 28
   Our First Kiss 29

Leo the ManLion
   Your Touch 33
   Our Sanctuary 34
   Sixty Magical Days 35
   A Night In Outer Space 37
   My Commitment 40
   My Tears 42
   What Are We Gonna Do 44
   Your Silence 45
   Promises 47
   Please Treat Me Like You Care 48

The Bandit and the Rose
   The Bandit's Warning 53
   The Bandit and the Rosebush 55
   The Diamond Rose In My Heart 57

The Bandit Stole My Heart Away 61
Your Heart You Say? 62
The Blossom Has Waned 65
The Grizzly Goddess 67
Love Is Like A Rose 68
The Goddess's Web 69
My Spirit Longs For Your Embrace 72

PEN Pals
No More Illusions 75
3rd Degree Burns 76
Heart On Ice 77
The Dance of Intimacy II 81
I'll Make Your Dreams Come True 82
The Juices Flow 83
Best Of Friends 84
My Heart is Lost to You 85
This Single Bed 86

Eve and the Serpent
You Planted the Seed 89
I Cried… 91
The Avocado 92
Bitten by the Serpent 93

Postscript 95
About the Author 97

Foreword

Dance of Intimacy provides the reader the opportunity to witness the birth of a soul. Linda's words open a window to peer through, allowing the reader to feel her anguish and her joy as she walks us through decades of yearning to be heard and seen in a world where love and loathing struggle to own her soul as she makes her way into the bright light of life.

I have known Linda since 1986 and have watched her grow into a wonderful woman and wonderful friend. Her work has power and the dimension that lay silent until the inner voice of a child yelled and rebelled to be set free.

Linda, may God continue to bless us with your words and to be an inspiration for others whose voices lay deep inside waiting for an opportunity to be heard and seen.

With admiration and joy of a job well done.

Val Clemont

Preface

The more I've lived life and studied literature, the more it becomes apparent that neither exists in a vacuum. Both literature and life are expressions of the interaction between the Creator and the created.

Writing poetry has been a cathartic process for me all my life. These words you read were never written with the intention of ever been shown to another human being. They are the words of one woman's perspective of the human condition in searching for love and intimacy.

I hope you, dear readers, will find yourselves upon these pages and be comforted that you are not alone — in your search for love — in your hurt from love, and hopefully too — in finding and keeping everlasting love in these exciting and changing times.

Linda Wall

September, 2007

Acknowledgments

Grateful acknowledgement goes to my Muse—the Poet Fairy—who stuck with me when my heart was breaking, and when my heart was overflowing with love & gratitude. She channeled through me to write the poems upon these pages.

I would also like to acknowledge the following for their input and suggestions after reading the first draft of this manuscript: Cara Beckett, Val Clemont, Donna Crossman, Pat DiFrancesco, Patti Dyson, Dan Morin, Don Presland, Loyd Suel, Ted Von Riessen, Steve Warm, and my daughter Carrie Wall. Your feedback helped shape this book into a smooth-flowing order—thank you from the bottom of my heart.
A special thank you to David DiFrancesco for helping with the cover design.

Linda

A Word Before

Behind every poem
there's a story that you may never know
   a story that may never be told.

My poems are a snapshot
encaptured a moment in time.
Just a glimpse
   a blink in time
into the depths
of My Heart
        My Soul
              The Universe
                    The Is.

The mindlessness of a genius.
The madness of a fool.

The talent is a curse,
   a cross I must bear.

The Dance of Intimacy

The Dance of Intimacy

Come dance the Dance of Intimacy with me.

Remember the times when our hearts,
      and souls danced and soared
           in perfect rhythm and harmony?
We danced the Dance of Intimacy.

Let's look back
      What do we see?

We had God.
We had Love.
We had Truth
      and Honesty.

That's the Dance of Intimacy.

Intimacy cannot exist without all of these,
For each of these is the other.
Together they can put no man asunder.
This is the Dance of Intimacy.

Come dance the Dance of Intimacy with me.

Remember the times when our hearts,
      and souls danced and soared
           in perfect rhythm and harmony?
We danced the Dance of Intimacy.

We had God.
We had Love.
We had Truth
      and Honesty.

Come dance the Dance of Intimacy with me.

I'm Afraid

I'm afraid to look around me
   afraid of what I might see.

Fears of intimacy,
   fears of being me.

Fearing of being alone,
   fearing one to call my own.

Afraid to look
   afraid to pray
   afraid one will come
         and finally stay.

Afraid of being alone
   afraid of finally being found.

Will you like me?
Will you hate me?
   Will you too eventually go away?

Choices In The Garden

Lust is the American Beauty
   growing in the flower garden.

She stands proud
   and tall   and dignified
dressed in red velvet
   splashed in heavenly scent.
She entices him
   bewitches him
to pluck her for his very own.

He bends down to admire her beauty
caresses her velvet gown
   inhales her fragrant scent.
Before he knows it
   she's pierced his heart
         drawn blood running down.
He's tangled in her thorny arms.
   He struggles.
   He scratches.
   He claws his way out
       of her greedy clutch.

He looks fondly over at
Love's little face-flower.
   the shy, quiet pansy
       standing alone in the corner.

Her purple velvet gown
and sunny yellow face
   sadly looking up at him.

Why could he not see?

I'm So Tired

Searching   searching
     searching everywhere I go.
Looking for a pair of arms to call my own.
Silent sadness burns and sears my bleeding soul.

Longing   longing
     emptiness abounds.
The pit of my soul deep,
     and darkness surrounds.

Crying   crying
     rivers of tears overflow
     engulfs my heart — my body — my soul.

Testing   testing
     sin all around.
Resisting   resisting
     resisting temptation.
Waiting for the true love I've never found.

I'm tired now.
     I'm not that strong.
I'm tired of waiting
     for my one true love to come along.
I'm tired of resisting the tests.

I'm tired of being alone.
I'm tired of the emptiness
     the loneliness all around.

Please God — I beg of You
     please send me a true love of my own
         One oh so true.

Patience is not my forte.
Where is my reward for following Your way?

'Patience   patience my little one.
A lifetime of pain will be undone.

Patience   patience my little one.
I'm preparing you to meet my son.
In a little while you both will smile
as you walk together in the sun.'

This Robed Gift

I sit here alone night after night
in my Serenity Cave
keeping the home fires burning bright.
Candles and incense glow in the window
of the Altar
     the Shrine to Serenity
          to all Sacred Things.

Guarding my Womanly Sacred Space
waiting to unveil this Robed Gift
     and lay it before the Altar of Love
for that special man
     the one Soulmate from Above.

I'm tired of having this
Womanly Sacred Space
violated and despoiled
     by the lust and the violence
of the rapists and the pillagers
from the days of old.

So I wait
     and wait
guarding my Womanly Sacred Space
     waiting to unveil this Robed Gift
and lay it before the Altar of Love.

Offers come by men
who want to partake in
My Sacred Womanly Delights
     but the timing
          or the person
just doesn't feel right.

So
      I sit alone night after night
here in my Serenity Cave
keeping the home fires burning bright.
Candles and incense glow in the window
of the Altar
      the Shrine to Serenity.
          to all Sacred Things.

Guarding my Womanly Sacred Space
waiting to unveil this Robed Gift
     and lay it before the Altar of Love
for that Special Man
    that one Soulmate from Above.

How much longer do I have to wait
and keep this Sacred Space sacred
before I unveil this Robed Gift
and lay it before the Altar of Love
   for that Special Man
      that one Soulmate from Above?

Teddy Bears

Teddy bears never let me down
   they always stick around.

Teddy bears have the hairy chest
   that I desire in a man.

Teddy bears don't run away
   no matter what I do or say.

Teddy bears are always there
   for my problems to share.

Teddy bears let me hug and squeeze
   so tight they can't breathe
      and cry on their shoulders too.

Teddy bears don't get mad
   or criticize what I say or do.

Teddy bears always stick around
   no matter what I say or do.

I think I'll look for a Teddy bear
   instead of a man

      next time 'round.

The Friendship Candle

The flame on the friendship candle
is beginning to wane
        and flicker
                and dim.

The wick grows long
    too long unattended
without love
    'n' care
             and attention.

Too much time passes
between our meetings
and greetings.

More and more dishonesty and lies
separate the truth
and the closeness between me 'n' you.

The flame on the friendship candle
is beginning to wane
        and flicker
                and dim.

The Friendship
        candle
          is
                snuffed
                      out . . .

The Heart Is A Betrayer of the Mind

The Heart is a betrayer of the mind
This Heart has a will of its own — not mine.
I can't stop loving you
You can't stop loving your heart's love true
    not me.

What in the world do I do?
My Heart loves you so true
    you love another — it's true.

My mind says it'll never be
    a true love between you 'n' me.
My Heart says it's already a reality.
but in all reality
    you think of her
        long for her
when you're with me.

I pray for my Heart to set you free
so that you may follow your own destiny,
but it just won't listen to me
    and the logic of my mind.

The Heart is a betrayer of the mind.
This Heart has a will of its own — not mine.

Pain Filled Soul

Pain filled soul
   scarred and seared
from old flames burnt out.

These are the choices I see
right in front of me.

To light the candle
on the new-flame-to-be
Risk once again
getting burned by carrying the torch

  OR

Painful loneliness
searching 'til the ends of my days
for the one-and-only Soulmate
I already let get away.

What would the Master do?
What is His Great Plan?

Do you really think He'd plant this seed
deep in our minds
   'n' hearts
        'n' souls
only to say,

'It was all a joke,
  how foolish you all can be!
Fools! You are all so deceived!'

My Erotic Fantasy

Breasts swollen with longing
    heaving with desire
for one I can not have.

Arms craving to be touched
by your sun-tanned hands.

Body screaming to be grazed
by puddles of sapphire blue
surrounded by life-etched laugh lines
enfolded in depths of mystery.

Longing to be caressed and sipped
by your ruby red lips
hidden 'neath a soft moustache.

But in all reality this is not to be,
so I have to be content with my erotic fantasy.

Our First Kiss

New lovers
    exploring slowly

Taking baby steps along the way
    a few phone calls
        dinner and a movie
            even a football game too,
holding hands a time or two
    talking and exploring possibilities
of a lifetime with you.

The day comes for our first kiss
    not planned or gauged and contrived,
just a quick peck in a spontaneous moment
    of hearts meeting soul of the other.

So fleeting and light
    quick little flutters
like a hummingbird
    flitting   about
we keep coming back for more
    another taste
        another test.

Soft smooth   lips   lite gently
    like velvety butterfly wings
caressed by a spring breeze.

Another day
    another hour
my lips keep coming back for more.

Each kiss a little longer

a little more brave and exploratory

tasting the nectar of you.

Each kiss conveying
my curiosity   and desire
             to know more of you.

Leo the ManLion

Your Touch

Your touch has
awakened my body
from a long, deep sleep.

My body tingles and
    throbs
        and twitches
at the memories of you.

My skin jumps
at thoughts of your touch.

My breasts swell,
    my heart beats fast
        hoping to see you
           again
                at last.

Every waking hour of my day,
    my body quaked
        hoping for release
           today.

Our Sanctuary

Crisis and chaos is the norm in our lives.
Some days it seems
we'll never claw our way out.
We come together
and lock the world out.
A Sanctuary in the storm of life.
A Safe Haven against the
daggers and arrows
slung in anger and pain.

You've got your crises and I've got mine.
We have to deal with them alone,
as the other stands by
    helplessly
        in prayer
            and silent strength.

When we come together
we lock the world out
of our Sanctuary against the storms of life.

Our Relationship
is what makes my life worthwhile.
It cushions the blows and softens the pain
    knowing I can come to you
        and be in your arms again.
They are my Sanctuary
against the storms of life.

Sixty Magical Days

All my life
searching and searching.
Like a lost soul
    being loved my only goal.
I gave up.
I surrendered.
I accepted myself
    and being alone.

Like the elusive butterfly that won't be caught
while being chased,
    You landed softly by my side
when I wasn't looking.
    You said,
      'I like where you're going;
        can I come along for the ride?'

We've been to   the Haunted House
    and dug up the skeletons
that have been buried for years.
We've been to   the Fun House
with its warped and twisted
    and crazy mirrors.

You've seen me cry rivers of salty tears.
Never this much fun,
    nor this much pain
in all our lonely years.

We've been to Hell and back.
We met on our journey to Heaven.
We've been to Mars
    and to the moon and

to Outer Space.

We've lived in a time warp where
hours have become days
and a month seems like seconds.

We've loved and laughed
and cried and growed
      trudging together down this rocky road.

Thanks for these sixty magical days.
Wanna try for   a record   and
double our fun?
Let's shoot for
      a hundred and twenty-one.

One Day at a Time

      of course.

A Night In Outer Space

　　　Rockets on the launch pad as the night closes
　in and　　blackness all around.

The rocket stands proud,
　　　whitely
　　　　　and rigid
　　　　thrusting towards the sky.

The world blackens as the pilot lights are lit.
Streams of white steam
　　　froth
　　　　　　and boil
at the base.

Red flares go off.

Thrusters thrusting.

　　　Booster power boosting.

　　　　　A shrinking sensation.

A sense of implosion before the big explosion.

　　　Ground breaking.

　　　　　　Earth shaking.

　　　The rocket tower
　　　throbs
　　　　　　and shakes
　　　　　　　　and sways.

LIFT OFF!

      And
           we're
                  on
                        our
       way
              to
                      Outer
                            Space!

Blackness all around.

Shooting stars rush past.

Fireworks exploding
   in a crazy kaleidoscope of color.

   Souls sailing into Outer Space.

Hovering and dipping
over the horizon
     and past the Milky Way.

Holding hands
    riding through the air

a nod
    a wink
        and we change direction.

Where we go we have no care.

   Breaking through the Black Hole
      to brightness
          and brilliance in the heavens above.

Soaring into heaven.

   Feeling God's sweet love
softly surround
         and caress us
         in our nightly journey,
brings tears of Joy
     and Awe
        and Gratitude
            to my eyes.

Come with me my darling
        to the nightly skies.

My Commitment

Through all our pain and tears and troubles,
nothing mattered except being together
      our hugs and cuddles.

You're going away.
I won't beg you to stay.
You've got to do what you must.

This doesn't have to be the end.
It can be a brand new beginning
just another stage
in our continued growth.

My life is in God's hands
and yours is too.

Whatever will be
    will be.
And God will see us through.

If we want to see this relationship
continue and grow,
   then we have to make a commitment
      and let each other
          and God   know.

For my part
I'm willing to take the risk.

It's a new challenge
    one I'm willing to take on.

It doesn't seem fair to me
that the last four months is all we'll have.

We made it through
      individually and together too
          so much pain
              and trouble
                    and tears.

Don't we get to be together
through the rewards and riches
      of the coming years?

Well I don't know
      I have no answers left.
          I will not run.
      I will not chase,
      but I may follow
         if asked.

But I am committed
to turn this over and see it through
      whatever that means to you.

My Tears

The tears I shed tonight
are my pain
    created by hanging onto that
which I have no right to hang onto
        you.

Be assured my love,
when my tears have dried up and gone away,
I will open my hands
    palms turned up
        and let you
            and your Soul
                slowly slip away.

You have your own journey
and appointment with Destiny to keep.
My love for you is that you will
find and reach
    your Highest Good
that you may find
    Serenity,
        Peace of mind
            and most of all
                yourself.

'Us' and our memories will have to be
put on the shelf only to be brought out
to warm us on   those long, cold
lonely days.

We can take the memories and lessons
    to brighten our Way.

May God,

and Love

    and Peace
bless you and comfort you along your way.

What Are We Gonna Do?

Only a little while ago
Our Love was elevated
to a Spiritual Plane
and philosophical talks.
And now it's earth-bound
      in Life's hard knocks.

The walls of anger and silence
you're building
      get higher
while I build mine too.

This isn't spiritual
and the love can't get through.

What are we gonna do?

Your Silence

I listen to your silence
and this is what it tells me
    either you're dead
        or dying
or you're torqued with me
and you're throwing a
childish temper tantrum
    to get your own way.

The latter I believe
    and games I won't play.

You say I never listen and assume too much
well I'm listening
to the silence
    'cuz you're not here to touch.

Your silence screams
of anger
    rage
        jealousy
            suspicion
ego
    arrogance
        and pride.

It brings with it defiance
    and hostility
with the morning's angry tide.

    I'm not talking,
    I'm listening,

but you don't say a word.

How do you expect to ever be heard
when you don't say a word,
        but let anger scream
                in the silence?

Promises

Promises never made can never be broken
so you say.

To never say those little words
'*I promise*'
doesn't make one much of a man,
if one can never count on you unless
you say those little words
'*I promise,*'
which so rarely pass your lips.

They say a man is as good as
his word . . .

Please Treat Me Like You Care

When we first met, you'd hold me close,
and run your fingers through my hair.
Now it doesn't seem like you even care.

You never comment, or even seem to notice
when I style or cut my hair.
Now it doesn't seem like you even care.

In the beginning we used to sit close,
and have long philosophical talks
while watching the setting sun.
Now it doesn't seem like you even care.

We used to sit close in the car,
and hold hands everywhere we went.
Now it doesn't seem like you even care.

Now, when we go out,
we could be strangers walking down the road.
It just doesn't seem like you even care.

I feel like   now
you figure that you've 'picked me'
there's nothing left for you to do.

I feel like a pretty rose
in a vase for all the world to view,
Or
   like the potted plant
   sitting upon my shelf
screaming for some
       water
         some nurturing
            and some sun.
And now it doesn't seem like you even care.

Do not ignore me and put me upon the shelf
until you're free, or
    when you want, or
        need me.
I want to be treated special.
Please treat me like you care.

Please treat me like you care.
Hold me close again.

Run your fingers through my hair once more.
Let's go for a walk and watch the setting sun.

Please share with me
the things you
    think
        and feel
            and do.

I want flowers
and inexpensive gifts,
        and cards for *'just because.'*
I want to be treated special.
Please treat me like you care.

Just as children and flowers,
    and pets and puppies
    need nurturing and
        tending
            and water and sun,
so too does this relationship, if
our hearts and souls are to beat as one.

Please treat me like you care,
      or in the morning
           there could be just one.

The Bandit and the Rose

The Bandit's Warning

(Caution—falling in love with criminals can be hazardous to your psyche!! It will embark you on an unforgettable spiritual journey!!)

I don't want your money; I don't want your car, or the things that you possess,
I want your love, your secret-self
    the things not known to others
        your special sweet caress.

I know you're scarred—you've been hurt before,
    but I'm slippery and fast
I'll steal your heart and your love.
Your heart will open—I'll walk right in
    and shut the door,
Before you know it you'll be head over heals
    in Agape love,
'Cause when Bandit steals a heart he goes to the Core!

It's true I come with all the problems known to Man, but baby if you can't help fix me, then who the hell can?
This silly game of life has left its scars on all of us
    that's true,
But these three days in the Can have made me realize just how close I've grown to you,
I've learned not to make promises I can't keep,
I've learned—it's true—we reap what we sow,
And those lessons cost me dearly, dear
    they weren't cheap!!!

One thing I can promise is a spiritual journey you'll never forget,
    'Cause my Father

he's promised me these things in His Book, so let's open
it together, let's check it out
      let's do it together, let's take a look!!!

The promises are sure, the Word is true
the Author's the God of Love,

He sent the Spirit to my Lord and Master — Jesus — in the
form of the dove.

So let me warn you darlin'
I may not be much but a rough ol' French Bandit,
but I'm gonna get your love!!!

Albert Lee Miller
a.k.a. - Bandit

The Bandit and The Rosebush

The Bandit sat down beside the Rosebush.
He was hidden in a spiritual disguise.

He told the Rosebush,
'You have such beautiful eyes.
May I sit with you a while?
    I want to see you smile,
I can tell it's been a while.
I see the hurt and pain in your eyes.
I'm a master of disguises,
And I'm gonna steal your heart away.'

The Rosebush replied,
'Don't forget – Bandit
    with the roses comes the thorns.
I don't want to hurt you,
But that's the way the Lord has made me.
With my beauty,
    with my scent,
I can also hurt you with my thorns.
With one tiny little prick
I can make your heart bleed all over
the streets of this big ol' town.

I know you – Bandit
Some days you dress up like a clown,
    other days you can be so sweet.

Bandit –
    Right now I'm sittin' at your feet.
Stop a while
    Admire my beauty

Inhale my fragrant scent,
But just be careful —
And remember that you've been warned,

If you try to pluck the Rosebush
Be careful of the thorns.'

The Diamond Rose In My Heart

I see these rosebushes growin' on the sides
of the wall,
They've become proud and haughty,
    or else I have
        and I can't hear their call!

There's one miles away though who's a Diamond Rose,
I caught a glimpse one morning of her beauty in a pose.
She's found a secret place in my heart
I've been the victim of Cupid's dart!
So now me — the fool — sittin' and walkin'
    and dreaming of her in the Can!!!

She drove me around in her Faithmobile
Me — the Bandit,
    and her at the wheel.
I was being myself — honest and twisted.
    I tried to scare her away.
Once — got so honest the fear took its grip.
She accepted it and got honest herself
    my heart it did slip!!!
In my heart, for her — I really do care
I'm really trying at times to deny,
    it's really not at all fair!

That Cupid — he's ruthless
always hits that spot, the little sadist
he gets things 'boilin' red hot'!
Yep it's got to be a laser
    a micro-beam-dot.

Doesn't he know that the Heart and Spirit
    they are intertwined?

Of course he does   the little bugger
hits your heart with Passion's arrow
his face lights up — he begins to shine.
If I could see him and grab him
    I'd wring his neck.

Aaah — it's not his fault — it was that glimpse
    of the panties — the Rosebush's attire
that's makin' me the wreck!!!

Yep — I'm puttin' the blame all on you,
This way Cupid's safe, I can fantasize
and stay thinkin' of your cute little pose
wanting to dress you in the finest silk lace!!!
Can't do it here sittin' in the Can
Yep — that's me baby — 'Bandit'
    Can I be your Man??

What I am — I am
    it may not be much
I may look to you as my safe-person-to-trust,
I'd run my tongue through your clusters
    and over your bust.

I may be a fool and not much at that
but baby I'm a sneaky ole bandit and quick as a cat!!!

Would you run the race,
    the quest for the prize?
With the foolishness of God we can
confound the wise!!!

Yes — Programs have answers,
but what's the right way?
It's the Word (Jesus), Father — Son and Holy Ghost!

He knew about us from the beginning of time.
He knows Bandit's kinky little heart's
    twisted, scarred and confused.
He knows baby that you come on strong
and slay dragons — the Goddess Warrior you are.
If I knew how   I'd serenade you
singing this in a song on the guitar.

Well Rosebush — you're part of the
Diamond Ring now deep in my heart.
Let's run to Love's deepest clusters of time
'You know eternity isn't even time
        it JUST *IS*!!!!'

Darling grab that phrase
    it's from God's Spirit
hot off the press!!!

But Bandit — the silly foolish ole thief
has he found a place fit for your caress??
The Fantasies — the Dreams — the Visions
    the Hope,
Run with me, my precious Diamond Rose
we will have time for the leather or lace.

Damn baby — I'm fallin' so fast!!!
I think you're the Warrior Woman
    the Goddess of Light,
so walk tenderly on and in and around
this ole Bandit's heart.
'Cause my first love — she ran
as you again were right — damn it!!!
Here I am pining away in the Can!!!
Stay away from the Yin and the Yang,
the intellectually, and politically correct
       the false cults, the sorcerers,

the devil's schemes.

I've made my choice
    now the ball's in your court,
so you have the Choice,
    the Power and Control,
      but I'm slippery Baby,
I warned you, I told you that I was hurtin' and proud.
I forget my armor — get hurt   and yet still am proud,
yet somehow I'm hopin' you'll love this ole fool,
I've won a lot of battles, but lost mega rounds
I'm not a quitter though — my faith's growing strong!!!

So seven's the number — I'm praying it won't be long
The ole heart's feelin' warm again
I'm knowin' you care!!!

I feel sorry for the person who comes between us
    'cause my buddy's from the army
      his specialty was explosives!

Together we will all run,
together we will stand!!
The Armour of God in the Spirit,
    and in the flesh!!!

So Rosebush make your choice
    let my heart rest.

Screw the pricks and the thorns
    Rosebush — you're the best!!!!

Bandit

The Bandit Stole My Heart Away

The Bandit stole my heart away
and we all must know that's a terrible sin.

How can the Goddess of Light
    slay her dragons down
        without her heart upon the sleeve of her gown?

She has no heart to wear upon her sleeve
for the Bandit is a goddamn thief.

I cannot slay no dragons down
        without no heart with which to live.
I need my heart — for passion it does give.

Bandit — please give me back my heart,
for it gives me the passion with which I must live.
I cannot slay no dragons down
        without no heart with which to live.

Your Heart You Say?

So you say I stole your heart away,
    my pretty Goddess of Light,
but what was that tender and wounded heart doing
sitting on your sleeve that cold and lonely night?

Even a Goddess needs rest you know.
The Warrior and dragons can't fight all the time,
'cause life's battles are incredible and we
need to stop and recover from the blows!

I must admit I'm really growing fond of this
tender beautiful heart,
and I warned you I was a thief
    right from the very start!!!

And now I've got these fantasies all going
through my head,
It would be so easy to use this situation to
try and manipulate you into my lonely bed.
That wouldn't be the gentlemanly thing to do
    that's one thing — of that I'm sure,
and this heart is very special,
even though a few times deeply cut.
But I tell ya Goddess — life with you
    can be awesome in a castle or a hut.

Yes I'll give you back your heart
    but only because you're so fine,
But damn it Rosebush — one thing you must do
    is give me back that heart of mine!!!

I'm not sure when you did it

whether it was the Coke bottle,
    or the glimpse
and now I know you're smiling
    thinking   it was such a cinch.

So now that we're both in possession
    of hearts taken in the passion-of-the-moment
how 'bout we come to some kind of consensus
    over — say — coffee and donuts??

Yes you got me where you want me
    you stole my heart clean away
I'm still not sure when it happened,
    and just like all the others,
I'm fearing you won't stay.

Well Goddess — darlin' I've got news for you
    it will come as a surprise
        there isn't any sex in Heaven
and I'm wanting to hear those
moans of pleasure   and those
    sensuous cries.

I hear and read how you put yourself down
    sometimes I get amazed
me — the Bandit with no heart
walkin' 'round thinking of you in a silly daze.

You won't be slaying dragons
    without a heart a Bandit can't steal
This is quite the dilemma — I'm in glue zone
    what's new — is it real?

    Now I'm scared to say *'I love you'*
    scared of your reaction.

You stole from a thief you crafty wench
What did you use as an attraction?

Well darlin' the words aren't coming now like
they can usually flow.

I'll risk it one more time

I do love you,

        but I'm wondering

how'd you get my heart

        'cause damn it

                I don't know!!!

Bandit

The Blossom Has Waned

Well Bandit

I think the fantasy has run its course
        in the light of day.
 A Bandit   always on the run
And a Rosebush sitting in the sun
      roots firmly planted in the ground.

I can't go to you,
      and you can't sit still long enough
to inhale the fragrance of the Rose.

The blossom has waned
      on this ol' Rosebush
in the light of day.
I can't walk with you
      and you won't stay.

This must be the end of the line
      for the Bandit
          and the Rosebush.

I'll stay rooted in the sun
      while you must go find
      and reconnect with the Son.

Bandit
  You'll always have
  a place in this ol' heart of mine.
Crazy Bandit
      who tried to steal my heart away,
but we gotta part the ways.

You don't want what I have to offer,
and you have nothing to me to give,
   so it's time to follow the Program
   and Live and Let Live.

The Grizzly Goddess

There was a Grizzly Goddess,
    with a heart of Gold,
the Bandit hurt her badly,
    but the story's not yet told.

The story and the chapters
    will be reviewed by some
but the Father's Will must be done.
The thorns came off the Rose and became
    as smooth as silk,
the love that they had together,
    the Heart's the house they built!!

Bandit

Love is like a rose

Love is like a rose that
never quits growing.

Truth is like a diamond that glitters
when the rays of the Son's light
sparks the quality within!

Your memory is that ray in my heart!

Bandit

The Goddess's Web

The Bandit's heart was cold and weak
    he'd sabotaged his love, and tasted defeat.
His faith was wavering from deep within
because he'd let the Goddess under his skin!!!!

This was illogical, irrational and it never made sense
He was the thief—so he thought,
    but something happened that couldn't
be bought.

A lady talked at a meeting one day
he was so angry at first he could hardly cope
soon after that—truth sparked through thoughts
    of dope!!!
He went back to the meeting and talked about the
broad.

She was nobody's fool,
    she quickly caught the play.
She confronted the Bandit, they began to become
    friends,
She was faithful to him again and again!!!

Soon he began to slip and slide,
But she would rescue the rascal and lay by his side.

He crawled deep within himself
he'd run with the coke and have the odd belt!

All his life he'd lost and run away from love,
    He was the jailhouse Christian
        that was laughed at and scorned!

But nothing ever touched him like this New-Age-dream
this cocky Grizzly Goddess — her eyes soft as a blue
summer's day.

She slipped right through the Con's last defense
        quick as the inmate scales the fence.
It couldn't — it wouldn't happen   to him!!!

All his life he'd ran and ran
        surprises for Bandit — the cops got him again!
No big deal — he's a man,   *'I can do the time!'*

He forgot the reality of the pus and the slime
He just gave up and slashed the Rose.

The thought he could walk away clean
The biggest crime ever committed took
place in Bandit's heart.

You see — the Goddess — she weaved her web
        around and through his Soul.
The Bandit would cry, pray and hope
    so down in the Hole!

But the Winner's the Loser who never
        quits trying,
the Goddess she had him
        no sense in denying!!!

He will wait for her day after day
he's getting stronger — yet weaker
        and filled with remorse,
He has a dream in his heart
but needs her again to chart the course.

So darlin' — is it over? You finished?

Or are you unsure?
　Make a decision and give it careful thought.

　You maybe can't
　　　　I understand　　　it's your life.
　But no matter what happens
　I'll be your friend.

All my love
Bandit

My Spirit Longs For Your Embrace

My spirit longs for your embrace.

Though we've struggled with life hurts
in my mind's eye, I see the beauty in your face.

I may never again have the trust I once knew,
but the warring Angels and Me are fighting for You!!!

The heaviness lifting, the oppression gone.

My Goddess she's coming with beauty and lace.

My Father's called her through his Son's grace!!!
Oh she may struggle and fight in her Holy War.
She may think she's lost but God's Keeping Score!!!

Albert Lee Miller

PEN Pals

No More Illusions

My innocence has died
    it's lying on the ground.
All illusions were smashed
    laying at my feet.
No such thing as love
    a Soulmate of mine
just moments
    and moments
        of continuous time
in this life of mine.

I accept defeat — callous as that sounds.
It was all an illusion
    just one great big dream
        so real
            it seemed.

Thought I'd found him a time or two
    even thought he was you.
But it was all an illusion
    just another silly dream.

Today I woke up
    no more illusions
my dreams and innocence were smashed.
There is no Soulmate of mine
    never
        ever
from the beginning
    to the ending of time.

Third Degree Burns

Third degree burns still sear my body and soul
from my last old flame that burnt out two years ago.

I want to love you
        but I really don't know.
To risk love another chance
        to dance another intimacy dance
                to have it go up in flames
I don't know if I
        could survive the pain.

I know that's not the attitude to have about love

I guess it means I've got more healing to do
        before I'll ever be free
                to love you like I want to do.

Heart On Ice

My heart had been broken one too many times
    too far broken to ever mend.
I put it on ice.
Maybe — one day — the scientists'll have a cure;
otherwise it'll stay right here
        locked on ice
   frozen in time.
No way to repair it,
so I'll put it on ice
where it's so cold and frigid
no man'll ever go!

After a year or more on ice it began to thaw
        no will of mine could change its course.
Well now I'm in a real big skid.
This block of ice — this heart of mine
it began to thaw.
Others began to like what they saw.
They started gettin' close again.

There's one — a real special guy
he really caught my eye.
Spend lots of time just hangin' out
     got to be real good friends.

With him there's nothin'
I'm afraid to say or do.
The world stands still when I'm with him.
Lose all track or sense of time.

Came to me one day with news to share
he just really needed to talk to someone
you see he's really attracted to someone

says he
and he doesn't know how to tell her so.
I'm sittin' there with baited breath
*'Well just tell her
 then you and she'll both know'*
says I.

He whispers her name and says
 'What do I do?'
I fight the urge to cry.
I swallow the tears.
 *'Well just tell her
  then you and she'll both know.'*

We're buddies
We're chums
We have lotsa fun and laughs,
quiet times and
 rockin' times
Made love a time or two.
 There's nothin' for him I wouldn't do.

Came to me the other day
says, *'we both need a new place to stay,
how about let's go halfs
 you 'n' me
  we know we'll have lotsa laffs.'*

I said *'no
as much as that's all true,
 I can't live under the same roof as you
  not when I care so deeply about you
   and you're attracted to her.
It wouldn't be fair to me – or to you.'*

He looked at me with astonished,
hurt and bewildered eyes,
    He said, *'no – I understand.'*

But since that day of honesty
    that day I laid my mangled,
melted heart on the table
things between us are different now.
Things I can't explain or understand
    spends more time with me somehow,
but certain things aren't said.
I don't know what these changes mean.
I've tried to stay out of his bed
    to give him time to clear his head.

Well the other night things happened
that I never planned.
Went over – just to hang out.
    Had a great time.

Once again the world was locked out
before I knew it, we were in each other's arms
doin' what couples do
    a night of Magic
        a night of Heaven
a night I'll never forget.
I went farther than I've ever gone before
I unleashed Passion's roar.
Afterward in each other's arms were spent,
but I can't help but feel something's missin'
    something's not quite right.

No words were spoken of love
    or commitment
        or times of more

Just *'see ya later — take care.'*

I don't know if I'm one of many,
    or if he's forgotten about her,
but tonight I sit here all alone
while he has *'dinner with friends.'*

God help me!
Give me back this heart of mine!
Help me to put it back on ice
    to be frozen again
        until the ends of time.

The Dance of Intimacy 2

The Dance of Intimacy isn't
just about what we do between the sheets
    although that really is so sweet.

We do the Dance of Intimacy when you
chop the firewood for the campfire
    to warm my feet.

We do the Dance of Intimacy when
I clean up the tent
    and campsite for you.

We do the Dance of Intimacy
traipsing through the woods
    communing with nature
        just you 'n' me .

We do the Dance of Intimacy
through the twinkle in your eyes
    and my dimpled smile
over a rousing game of cards.

We do the Dance of Intimacy
with hugs and embraces.
For the Dance of Intimacy
can be seen on our faces
as we share each moment
    in time and space.

Come my darling
    won't you join me
in the Dance of Intimacy?

I'll Make Your Dreams Come True

You lie next to me
but you — I'm afraid to touch.
I want you.
    I believe you want me,
        or rather you did — once.

Lying next to me
    body naked and
        Ohhh
            so inviting.
I'm afraid to touch
    afraid to make my move.
I'm afraid you'll laugh at me
    and in the morning — scorn.

So I lay awake
dreaming of your sweet caress
    never to have my fantasy
fulfilled.

So if this is a dream,
    never let me wake.
If this is a nightmare,
    please give me a shake.
And if this be your fantasy too,
    then please tell me
and I'll make your dreams come true.

The Juices Flow

There's something about
two in the afternoon
on a hot summer day
that turns me on
    Makes the juices flow!

The thought of your
hot-cold body next to mine
glistening with sweat and matted hair.
That turns me on!
    Makes the juices flow!

A cold winter night
when the blood in my veins
has turned to ice,
to lay next to you
and absorb your body's heat.
That turns me on!
    Makes the juices flow!

Let's face it!
Let's get honest!
    You turn me on!
You make the juices flow!
That's what turns me on!
    Makes the juices flow!

Best Of Friends

You say we are the best of friends
    buddies through thick and thin
        that with me you can share so much
then why do you shut me out
    and lock yourself within?

You say you don't want to be a burden
    to bother others with your troubles
        but — hey
that's what being friends is all about.

No — this week
    You're not a friend to me
        for you won't allow me a friend to be.

You
    control this friendship
      and the level of intimacy
        by your silence and isolation
your rational lies
    your care and concern to spare me
      to not a burden to be
but it's all bullshit
    and self-centered macho male-ego, false pride.

No — this week
    You're not a friend to me
        for you won't allow me a friend to be.

This Single Bed

This single bed that we share
may as well be a
      king
           or queen size
for the chasm between us there.

No touching allowed.
      no cuddles.
           no good night kiss
  no nightly bliss.

Back-to-back we lay. . .

My Heart Is Lost To You

My heart is lost to you
and I don't know how it happened
or what I should say or do.

You say you're going away.
My heart and body
silently scream for you to stay.

My words assure you
that your leaving is okay,
    if that's what you gotta do
for I have no right to ask you to stay.
    I have nothing to offer you
Except this ol' heart on my sleeve.

Eve and the Serpent

You Planted the Seed...

You planted the seed of desire for you in my stony heart.

You patiently tilled the soil for many months
by befriending me with your patient smile,
    and strong and reassuring hugs.
You never crowded my space, but
    always let me see you around.

You planted seeds of longing for your kisses
long before the act just by hugging and
putting your lips ever so close and withdrawing
without a hint of any romantic intentions.

As my stony heart became more pliable beneath your
skilled hands, you came closer and started hanging
'round some more.

You even kissed me—chastely, but
it was 'only a Christmas kiss between two friends.'

A perfect gentleman.
    A gentle man you remained.

You danced with me and called me pretty names
    like Beautiful and Princess...

You made it hard for a girl to resist
    even one with a stony heart like mine!

Your kisses became more exploring
        more passionate too.
I started thinking about the possibilities
between me 'n' you, but
        I still resisted — for a little while.

It wasn't your charm I was resisting though
        it was the many differences between us
that I could not see my way through.

Your patient tilling of my mind
talking of Love and Spirituality
        of books and History
broke through any resistance left in me.
I finally surrendered to *what will be…*

And now you say you need your space,
that I'm reading too much into all of this,
and that you only want to be *just friends…*

Well if that is the way that it **has** to be…

You see,
I cannot make you love me, or
be anywhere other than where you be.
so if it's *just friends* you want,
then *just friends* I will be…

For now you've plucked the tender seedlings,
these little sprouts of Love's blossom
right out from my heart and trampled them down
…never to grow and blossom into the
fragrant bouquet of Love for another day.

I Cried

I cried for me
I cried for you
I cried for what could be…

The Avocado

The Avocado is ripened
      awaiting the thrust of your Sword
to split it open and
remove the hard bitter pit lodged deep within
in order that you may
      see   and taste
its succulent delights.

The firm and creamy smooth flesh
      ripened under Love's radiant heat
these long winter months
      has blossomed and ripened
for your delighted picking.

Enjoy the Avocado
      suck the sweet flesh to your delight
for you have tended and nurtured Her
      in your Garden of Love.

Bitten by the Serpent

You slithered ever so slowly
into my line of vision
    then hypnotized me with
your spellbinding gaze
and   love-dance   from a distance
    so as to not frighten me away.

You sat still and patiently in
Our Garden of Love,
shaking your tantalizing
Rattlers of Love until
little Eve approached the deadly Snake.

We danced in Our Garden
becharming and bewitching one another
with our magic charms
    trying to seduce the other
to bite the forbidden fruit.

Just as little Eve was
about to take a bite,
you struck a deadly blow.
You bit little Eve with
your Serpent fangs
and allowed your venom to flow.

Two weeks your poison
has been coursing 'neath her skin.
Your venom has spread
everywhere beneath her skin.

Last night the fevers came.

She lay beneath the covers
throbbing and thrashing from the pain
of your venom coursing everywhere.
Dreams and hallucinations of you
and your hypnotic spell tortured her dreams.

She cried out for release:
To be relieved of her pain!

   Her fever!

       Her itch!

There's only one cure from
the bite of a poisonous snake,
and that is to be injected
with the Venom of the Serpent.

Postscript

I find it very interesting that the last poem in this series takes us back to Eve and the Serpent in the Garden of Eden — where life — and intimacy — all began.

This suggests to me that I have come full circle.

In Native American tradition, it is said that life is a dance on the circle — or hoop — of life. Others suggest that life is played out on parallel planes simultaneously. I envision a combination of these beliefs — that life is more like a *Slinky*™ toy stretched out. When one travels the 'circle' and returns to the beginning, they have actually *elevated* a notch on the circle of life.

This collection represents for me my personal evolution on the hoop of life — one full revolution. Now my life moves into a new phase, slightly elevated from where this all began. Hopefully it represents the same for you.

To future possibilities — in life — in love — and in intimacy.

Linda Wall

October 2007

About The Author

Linda Wall was awarded the distinction as **'Poet of Merit'** by the International Society of Poets in 1995 and 2002. She has had a few of her poems published in anthologies compiled by the International Society of Poets.
Linda was also nominated 'Poet of the Year' for 2002 by the Famous Poets Society.

Linda has written over 200 poems during the last 25 years. This is her first published collection of poetry.

Ms. Wall resides in *'Beautiful British Columbia'*, Canada and has one grown daughter.

Linda is a freelance writer, and independent researcher.

A note from Linda's Daughter

Mom was working on getting her second book of poetry published in early 2024. In July 2024 she was diagnosed with stage 4 cancer. Mom passed away in September 2024.
I am working on having her second book published for early 2026.
Please watch for Contemplations by Linda Wall.
∽ Carrie ∽